EVERY LIFE MATTERS

每一個生命的事項

Chinese: EVERY LIFE MATTERS

كل المسائل الحياة

Arabic: EVERY LIFE MATTERS

Kila Mambo Maisha

Swahili: EVERY LIFE MATTERS

כל החיים הוא חשובים

Hebrew: EVERY LIFE MATTERS

すべてのライフ事項

Japanese: EVERY LIFE MATTERS

Cada Vida es importante

Spanish: EVERY LIFE MATTERS

toute vie est important

French: EVERY LIFE MATTERS

alles Leben ist wichtig

German: EVERY LIFE MATTERS

Каждая жизнь Вопросы

Russian: EVERY LIFE MATTERS

Ogni Matters Vita

Italian: EVERY LIFE MATTERS

Cada vida importa

Portuguese: EVERY LIFE MATTERS

EVERY LIFE MATTERS

(English)

Hello Boys and Girls!

I want you to sit up straight take a deep breath, and get ready to hear the coolest story of your life.

Ever wonder why the Sun shines on you?

And why the Moon stares at you at night?

Well let me tell you, it's because every life matters.

Yes that means you boys and girls!

Let's not forget, human life matters but the Sun and Moon is there for all living things. This includes trees, plants, small animals even the little birds.

ALL living things.

Every Life Matters!

Well if every life matters, why are humans so mean to one another?

That's because boys, and girls many humans do not yet fully understand the simple truth that the Sun and the Moon know. That is

Every Life Matters!

I want you today to reach for the stars, and know that when you make it there, you will be surrounded by a Universe that knows Every Life Matters!

So when you come back
to this beautiful planet,
teach those you meet
with a smile that says

Every Life Matters.

Acknowledgements

I would like to thank all the artist who illustrated the clip art thus making a contribution which is helping to make this world a better place.

Remember to Live Well, and Be Kind to One Another!

www.ingramcontent.com/pod-product-compliance
Lightning Source LLC
Chambersburg PA
CBHW042334150426
43194CB00001B/51